THE YOUNG CHEFS GUIDE

Delicious and Healthy Recipes for Managing
Diabetes in Children and Adults

Author

DANIEL BERLIN

CONTENTS

INTRODUCTION

THE ROLE OF NUTRITION IN MANAGING DIABETES

Diabetes, a condition marked by elevated blood sugar levels, has become a global health concern. It's not just a medical issue but a lifestyle challenge too. The role of nutrition in managing diabetes is paramount, and understanding this relationship can empower individuals to take control of their health.

The Power of Diet in Diabetes Management

We often underestimate the power of diet in managing chronic conditions. For diabetes, it's a game-changer. A balanced diet can help maintain blood sugar levels, reduce the risk of complications, and even reverse the progression of the disease in some cases.

Key Dietary Strategies for Diabetics

What does a diabetic-friendly diet look like? It's not just about cutting out sugar. It involves a holistic approach that includes:

1. **Carbohydrate Counting**: Not all carbs are created equal. Complex carbohydrates like whole grains are beneficial, as they have a lower glycemic index and don't spike blood sugar levels quickly.

2. **Fiber-Rich Foods**: Fiber slows down glucose absorption, aiding in blood sugar regulation. Foods rich in fiber include fruits, vegetables, whole grains, and legumes.

3. **Healthy Fats**: Incorporating healthy fats from sources like avocados, nuts, and olive oil can help improve insulin sensitivity.

4. **Lean Proteins**: Proteins have a minimal impact on blood sugar levels. Opting for lean protein sources like chicken, fish, and plant-based proteins can be beneficial.

5. **Portion Control**: Overeating, even healthy foods, can lead to weight gain and increased blood sugar levels. Portion control is critical in managing diabetes.

The Impact of Nutritional Knowledge on Diabetes

Educating oneself about nutrition and diabetes is empowering. Knowing what to eat, how much to eat, and when to eat can make a significant difference in managing diabetes. Healthcare professionals often stress the importance of nutritional education as part of diabetes management.

CHAPTER 1

DIABETES AND NUTRITION BASICS FOR KIDS

1.1 WHAT IS DIABETES?

Diabetes, a term we often hear but may not fully understand. What is it? How does it affect our bodies? Let's delve into this topic and shed some light on this prevalent health condition.

Diabetes is a chronic health condition that affects how our bodies convert food into energy. When we consume food, most of it breaks down into sugar (glucose) and releases into our bloodstream. This increase in blood sugar signals our pancreas to release insulin. Insulin, often referred to as a key, allows the blood sugar to enter our body's cells for use as energy.

However, with diabetes, our body either doesn't produce enough insulin or can't use it as effectively as it should. This leads to an excess of blood sugar in` our bloodstream, which can cause serious health problems over time, such as heart disease, vision loss, and kidney disease.

Types of Diabetes

There are three main types of diabetes: type 1, type 2, and gestational diabetes.

- **Type 1 Diabetes**: This type is thought to be caused by an autoimmune reaction where the body attacks itself by mistake, stopping your body from making insulin. It can be diagnosed at any age, and symptoms often develop quickly.

- **Type 2 Diabetes**: With this type, your body doesn't use insulin well and can't keep blood sugar at normal levels. It develops over many years and is usually diagnosed in adults.

- **Gestational Diabetes**: This type develops in pregnant women who have never had diabetes. If you have gestational diabetes, your baby could be at higher risk for health problems.

1.2 TYPES OF DIABETES IN CHILDREN

Diabetes, a condition often associated with adults, is unfortunately not exclusive to them. It can affect children too, and the impact can be just as significant. Let's explore the types of diabetes that can occur in children and how they can be managed.

Diabetes in Children

Diabetes in children is a serious condition where the child's body is unable to properly process sugar (glucose) into energy. This results in an excess of sugar in the bloodstream, which can lead to long-term health complications. The two most common forms of diabetes in children are type 1 and type 2.

Type I Diabetes in Children

Type I diabetes, often diagnosed in children, is a condition where the body's immune system mistakenly attacks itself, stopping the production of insulin. It can occur at any age but is most commonly diagnosed between ages 4-6 and 10-143. Symptoms often develop quickly and require immediate medical attention.

Type 2 Diabetes in Children

Type 2 diabetes, once rare in children, has been increasing in frequency due to the rise in childhood obesity. In type 2 diabetes, the child's body doesn't use insulin effectively, leading to high blood sugar levels. It typically manifests after puberty, with the highest rate between ages 15-193.

Managing Diabetes in Children

Managing diabetes in children involves a combination of healthy eating, regular physical activity, and medication if necessary. Regular check-ups are crucial to monitor the child's blood sugar levels and to treat any complications early.

While diabetes in children can be challenging, it's important to remember that with the right care and management, children with diabetes can lead healthy, normal lives. As we continue to learn more about this condition, we can better equip ourselves and our children to tackle it head-on. Remember, knowledge is power, and understanding is the first step towards empowerment.

1.3 BALANCING BLOOD SUGAR LEVELS

In the hustle and bustle of our daily lives, we often overlook the importance of maintaining balanced blood sugar levels. But did you know that balanced blood sugar is a crucial aspect of overall health and well-being? Let's dive into this topic and explore how we can achieve this balance.

Blood Sugar

Blood sugar, or glucose, is the main source of energy for our body's cells. When we consume food, especially sugars and simple carbohydrates, these foods release glucose into the bloodstream very quickly, causing a spike in blood sugar. This spike stimulates the pancreas to produce insulin, which helps move the sugars from the bloodstream into the cells. However, if insulin levels are driven up repeatedly due to too much sugar in the blood, it can lead to increased abdominal fat, weight gain, unhealthy cholesterol levels, and eventually, type 2 diabetes.

Balancing Blood Sugar: Strategies and Tips

Balancing blood sugar levels involves a combination of a balanced diet, regular physical activity, and stress management. Here are some strategies to help you achieve this balance:

Glycemic Index: Foods low on the glycemic index release energy slowly into the bloodstream and cause only minor changes in blood sugar levels. These include animal protein, nuts and seeds, beans and lentils, whole grains, many vegetables, and some fruits.

Eat Balanced Meals: Eating three well-balanced meals per day is crucial to support blood sugar stability. To build a balanced meal, include all three macronutrients: protein, carbs, and fat.

Incorporate Blood Sugar-Lowering Foods: Several foods may help lower your blood sugar, including broccoli, seafood, pumpkin, nuts, okra, flaxseed, beans, fermented foods, chia seeds, kale, berries, avocados, oats, citrus, kefir, eggs, and apples.

Avoid Sugary Drinks and Snacks: Sugary drinks and snacks can cause a rapid spike in blood sugar levels. Opt for water, herbal teas, or unsweetened beverages instead.

Exercise Regularly: Regular physical activity can help lower blood sugar levels and increase insulin sensitivity.

Balancing blood sugar levels is not just about avoiding diabetes. It's about embracing a healthier lifestyle that will lead to improved energy levels, better mood, and overall well-being. Remember, every step you take towards balancing your blood sugar is a step towards a healthier you!

1.4 IMPORTANCE OF A WELL-BALANCED DIET FOR DIABETIC KIDS

When it comes to managing diabetes in children, the role of a well-balanced diet is paramount. It's not just about controlling blood sugar levels, but also about fostering overall health and well-being. Let's delve deeper into this topic.

Diabetes in Children

Diabetes in children is a condition where the child's body fails to efficiently convert sugar (glucose) into energy. This results in an excess of sugar in the bloodstream, which can lead to long-term health complications[2]. A well-balanced diet plays a pivotal role in managing these blood sugar levels and preventing complications.

The Role of a Balanced Diet

A balanced diet for diabetic kids is not about strict restrictions but about learning to make healthy choices. It's about balancing carbohydrates, proteins, and fats to keep blood sugars in a healthy range. A balanced diet can also help reduce the risks of developing chronic health conditions—such as type 2 diabetes—and weight issues such as obesity.

Components of a Balanced Diet

A balanced diet for diabetic kids should include:

1. **Proteins**: Lean meats, poultry, eggs, beans, soy products, nuts, and seeds.

2. **Fruits**: Fresh and frozen fruits are excellent sources of numerous nutrients.

3. **Vegetables**: A variety of different styles and colors throughout the week.

4. **Grains**: Whole grains are high in fiber and are a great source of energy.

5. **Dairy**: Aim for low-fat or fat-free options as sources of calcium.

CHAPTER 2

SETTING UP A DIABETIC-FRIENDLY KITCHEN

2.1 KITCHEN ESSENTIALS

Setting up a kitchen that caters to the needs of a diabetic child can seem daunting. However, with the right kitchen essentials and a bit of organization, it can become a manageable task. Let's explore how to set up a diabetic-friendly kitchen.

The Needs of a Diabetic Child

A diabetic child's diet needs to be well-balanced, ensuring they get the right nutrients while maintaining their blood sugar levels. This requires careful selection of food items and the right kitchen tools to prepare them.

Essential Kitchen Appliances

The basic list of kitchen appliances includes a fridge and stove. However, for a diabetic-friendly kitchen, you might want to consider a few more appliances:

1. **Oven**: For baking vegetables and lean meats.

2. **Fridge**: To store fresh fruits, vegetables, and lean proteins.

3. **Blender**: To make healthy smoothies and soups.

4. **Microwave**: For quick and easy meals.

Essential Cookware and Utensils

Having the right cookware and utensils can make cooking easier and more enjoyable. Here are some essentials:

1. **Non-Stick Skillet**: For low-fat cooking.

2. **Sauce Pan**: For making sauces and boiling vegetables.

3. **Roasting Pan**: For roasting meats and vegetables.

4. **Measuring Cups & Spoons**: For accurate portion control.

Stocking the Pantry

A well-stocked pantry is the backbone of a diabetic-friendly kitchen. Here are some essentials:

1. **Whole Grains**: Such as brown rice and whole-wheat pasta.

2. **Canned Beans**: A good source of protein and fiber.

3. **Canned Vegetables**: Choose no added salt options.

4. **Canned Tuna or Salmon**: Opt for those in water.

5. **Dried Herbs**: To add flavor without adding sodium.

Setting up a diabetic-friendly kitchen may require some effort, but the benefits are worth it. With the right tools and essentials, you can create a space that makes managing your child's diabetes easier and less stressful. Remember, every small step you take brings you closer to a healthier lifestyle for your child.

2.2 MUST-HAVE COOKING TOOLS FOR KIDS

Cooking is a valuable life skill that not only fosters creativity but also encourages healthy eating habits. Equipping kids with the right cooking tools can make their culinary adventures both safe and enjoyable. Let's explore the must-have cooking tools for kids.

Importance of Cooking Tools for Kids

Having the right tools can make a significant difference in a child's cooking experience. It can enhance their safety, boost their confidence, and make cooking more fun.

Essential Cooking Tools for Kids

Here are some must-have cooking tools for kids:

1. **Apron**: An apron is essential to protect their clothes from spills and splatters.

2. **Chef's Hat**: A chef's hat can make kids feel like a professional and get them in the mood to cook.

3. **Veggie Scrubber Gloves**: These gloves are perfect for little hands to easily scrub potatoes and other veggies.

4. **Non-Slip Mixing Bowls**: These bowls stay put, reducing the chance of spills.

5. **Kid-Friendly Knife Set**: A set of knives designed for kids can help them cut ingredients safely.

6. **Measuring Cups and Spoons**: These tools are essential for teaching kids about portions and measurements.

7. **Silicone Baking Mats**: These mats are great for baking and easy to clean.

8. **Cooking and Baking Set**: A comprehensive set can include a variety of tools like a rolling pin, whisk, spatula, and more.

Equipping kids with the right cooking tools is a step towards fostering their culinary curiosity and teaching them a valuable life skill. Remember, the goal is not just to teach them to cook, but to instill a love for cooking and healthy eating habits that will last a lifetime.

2.3 STOCKING A DIABETES-FRIENDLY PANTRY

Managing diabetes involves more than just monitoring blood sugar levels. It also requires a well-stocked pantry filled with diabetes-friendly foods. Let's explore how to stock a pantry that supports a healthy, balanced diet for individuals with diabetes.

Needs of a Diabetic Diet

A diabetic diet is not about strict restrictions but about making healthy and balanced food choices. It's about balancing carbohydrates, proteins, and fats to keep blood sugars in a healthy range. A well-stocked pantry can make meal planning and preparation easier and more efficient.

Essential Pantry Items

Here are some must-have items for a diabetes-friendly pantry:

1. **Whole Grains**: Foods like brown rice, whole-wheat pasta, and quinoa are nutritious and less likely to spike blood sugar levels.

2. **Canned Beans and Lentils**: These offer plant-based protein and fiber, and are great for diabetes-friendly meatless meals.

3. **Canned Vegetables**: Opt for no added salt options.

4. **Canned Tuna or Salmon**: Choose those in water.

5. **Dried Herbs**: These can add flavor without adding sodium.

6. **Olive Oil**: A heart-healthy fat that's great for cooking.

7. **Vinegars**: These can be used in combination with olive oil to create yummy dressings.

Stocking a diabetes-friendly pantry may require some effort, but the benefits are worth it. With the right foods on hand, you can create meals that are both tasty and supportive of blood sugar management. Remember, every step you take towards stocking a diabetes-friendly pantry is a step towards a healthier lifestyle.

2.4 SMART SNACKING OPTIONS

Snacking can be a double-edged sword. While it can help curb hunger and provide extra nutrients, the wrong snack choices can lead to weight gain and blood sugar spikes. Let's explore some smart snacking options that are both delicious and nutritious.

Smart Snacking

Smart snacking is about choosing snacks that pack a nutritious punch. It's about selecting foods that are rich in nutrients, low in unhealthy fats, and that can help regulate blood sugar levels.

Smart Snacking Options

Here are some smart snacking options to consider:

1. **Whole Grains**: Whole-grain snacks can give you energy with staying power. Try some whole-grain low-salt pretzels or tortilla chips, or a serving of high-fiber cereals.

2. **Fruits and Vegetables**: Fresh, frozen, canned (in 100% juice), or dried varieties are all good options[4]. Pair them with a small amount of protein or healthy fat for a balanced snack.

3. **Protein-Rich Foods**: Foods such as peanut butter, low-fat yogurt, or cheese are great sources of protein and can help keep you full.

4. **Nuts and Seeds**: Unsalted nuts and seeds make great snacks. They contain many beneficial nutrients and are more likely to leave you feeling full.

5. **Healthy Fats**: Foods like avocados and olives are rich in healthy fats and can be included in your snack options.

Smart snacking is an art that can be mastered with a little bit of knowledge and planning. By choosing the right foods, you can satisfy your hunger, boost your nutrient intake, and keep your blood sugar levels stable. Remember, every snack is an opportunity to nourish your body, so make it count!

CHAPTER 3

BREAKFAST DELIGHTS

3.1 NUTRITIOUS MORNING STARTERS

Starting your day with a nutritious breakfast can set the tone for the rest of the day. It can provide you with the energy you need, help regulate your blood sugar levels, and prevent overeating later in the day. Let's explore some nutritious morning starters that can help you kickstart your day the healthy way.

Importance of a Nutritious Start

A nutritious start to the day involves consuming foods that are rich in nutrients, low in unhealthy fats, and that can help regulate blood sugar levels. It's about selecting foods that provide a steady release of energy throughout the morning.

Nutritious Morning Starters

Here are some nutritious morning starters to consider:

1. **Hydrate with Warm Water:** Starting your day with a glass of warm water can help flush out toxins and hydrate your body.

2. **Soaked Nuts and Seeds:** These are a nutrient-rich start to the day, providing a good dose of healthy fats, protein, and fiber.

3. **Savory Breakfast Options:** Foods like sprouts, eggs, vegetables, or dal cheela are high in protein and fiber, making them a great start to the day.

4. **Porridge:** Opt for steel-cut oats with whole milk for a nourishing meal.

5. **Fresh Fruits**: Starting your day with fresh fruits can provide a quick energy boost and a good dose of vitamins and minerals.

6. **Greek Yogurt**: A scoop of protein-rich Greek yogurt can be a great addition to your morning meal.

Starting your day with a nutritious breakfast is one of the best things you can do for your health. It can provide you with the energy you need, help regulate your blood sugar levels, and set the tone for the rest of the day. Remember, every meal is an opportunity to nourish your body, so make it count!

3.2 DIABETES-FRIENDLY CEREALS AND OATMEAL

Breakfast is often hailed as the most important meal of the day, and for individuals with diabetes, this statement holds even more truth. Starting the day with a balanced, nutritious breakfast can help maintain stable blood sugar levels throughout the day. Let's explore some diabetes-friendly cereals and oatmeal options that can make your mornings brighter and healthier.

Importance of a Diabetes-Friendly Breakfast

A diabetes-friendly breakfast is not just about controlling blood sugar levels, but also about providing the body with essential nutrients for the day. Choosing the right cereals and oatmeal can make a significant difference in managing diabetes.

Diabetes-Friendly Cereals

When choosing cereals, it's important to look for options that are high in fiber and low in added sugars. Here are some diabetes-friendly cereals:

1. **Whole Grain Cereals**: Whole grain cereals like shredded wheat or bran are excellent choices as they are high in fiber and low in sugar.

2. **Cornflakes**: Opt for plain cornflakes rather than the sugar-coated or honey and nut varieties.

3. **Grape-Nuts**: Made from whole grain wheat flour and malted barley, these cereals are a good source of nutrients.

Diabetes-Friendly Oatmeal

Oatmeal is a great breakfast option for individuals with diabetes. Here are some tips for making your oatmeal diabetes-friendly:

1. **Choose the Right Type**: Opt for steel-cut oats or old-fashioned style oats as they have a lower glycemic index compared to instant oats.

2. **Avoid Added Sugars**: Instead of adding sugar, sweeten your oatmeal with fresh fruits or a sprinkle of cinnamon.

3. **Add Protein**: Adding a scoop of protein-rich Greek yogurt or a handful of nuts can make your oatmeal more filling and balanced.

Choosing the right breakfast cereals and oatmeal can make a significant difference in managing diabetes. It's all about finding the balance between taste and nutrition. Remember, every meal is an opportunity to nourish your body and manage your diabetes better. So, make your breakfast count!

3.3 SMOOTHIES AND BREAKFAST SHAKES

Starting your day with a smoothie or breakfast shake can be a delightful and nutritious way to kick start your morning. Packed with fruits, vegetables, and other nutrient-rich ingredients, these beverages can provide a quick and easy meal that's perfect for busy mornings. Let's explore some delicious and healthy options for smoothies and breakfast shakes.

Benefits of Smoothies and Breakfast Shakes

Smoothies and breakfast shakes can be a great addition to a balanced diet. They are quick to prepare, easy to consume, and can be packed with a variety of nutrients. Plus, they can be customized to suit individual tastes and dietary needs.

Delightful Smoothie Options

Smoothies are a fantastic way to incorporate fruits and vegetables into your diet. Here are some delightful smoothie options:

1. **Berry Blast Smoothie**: Packed with antioxidants, a berry smoothie with strawberries, blueberries, and raspberries can be a refreshing start to your day.

2. **Green Power Smoothie**: A blend of spinach, kale, and avocado, this smoothie is a powerhouse of nutrients.

3. **Tropical Delight Smoothie**: With mango, pineapple, and coconut water, this smoothie can transport you to a tropical paradise.

Breakfast Shake Delights

Breakfast shakes can be a great source of protein and other essential nutrients. Here are some breakfast shake delights:

1. **Protein-Packed Peanut Butter Shake**: With peanut butter, banana, and a scoop of protein powder, this shake can keep you full until lunch.

2. **Choco-Banana Breakfast Shake**: A blend of bananas, cocoa powder, and Greek yogurt, this shake is a healthy way to satisfy your chocolate cravings.

3. **Vanilla Almond Breakfast Shake**: With almond milk, vanilla protein powder, and a dash of cinnamon, this shake is both delicious and nutritious.

Smoothies and breakfast shakes can be a delightful and nutritious start to your day. They offer a quick and easy way to consume a variety of fruits, vegetables, and other nutrient-rich foods. So, why not give your day a delightful start with a smoothie or breakfast shake? Remember, a healthy day starts with a healthy breakfast!

3.4 CREATIVE EGG DISHES FOR KIDS

Eggs are a breakfast staple in many households. They're versatile, packed with protein, and can be transformed into a variety of delightful dishes. Let's explore some creative egg dishes that can make breakfast an exciting adventure for kids.

The Benefits of Eggs

Eggs are a powerhouse of nutrition, providing high-quality protein, vitamins, and minerals. They can be cooked in numerous ways, making them a versatile ingredient for creative dishes.

Creative Egg Dishes for Kids

Here are some creative egg dishes that kids will love:

1. **Egg Bagel Bites**: Mini bagels topped with scrambled eggs, cheese, and bacon make for a delightful and nutritious bite-sized breakfast.

2. **Classic Deviled Eggs**: These can be a fun and tasty snack. You can add a twist by using different fillings like avocado or tuna.

3. **Cauliflower Breakfast Muffins**: A delicious way to sneak in some veggies. These muffins are made with eggs, cauliflower, and cheese.

4. **Egg-In-A-Hole Buns**: A fun twist on the classic egg-in-a-hole toast. Kids will love the cute little breakfast buns.

5. **Ham Egg & Cheese Roll-Ups**: Who needs a tortilla when you have ham? This creative dish wraps scrambled eggs and cheese in a slice of ham.

6. **Eggo Breakfast Sliders**: Mini waffles filled with scrambled eggs and bacon. These sliders are just as fun to eat as they are to make.

7. **Breakfast in a Blanket**: This dish takes the classic pigs in a blanket and gives it a breakfast twist with eggs and cheese.

8. **Tater Tot Breakfast Bake**: This hearty dish combines tater tots, eggs, and cheese for a filling breakfast.

9. **Mini Breakfast Pizzas**: Who said you can't have pizza for breakfast? Top mini pizza crusts with scrambled eggs, cheese, and your kid's favorite toppings.

10. **Breakfast Grilled Cheese**: Take the classic grilled cheese sandwich and add scrambled eggs for a breakfast version.

11. **Egg, Avocado, And Cheddar Homemade "Hot Pockets"**: Stuffed with scrambled eggs, mashed avocado, and cheese,

these are a healthier alternative to store-bought hot pockets.

Eggs are a wonderful ingredient that can be transformed into a variety of creative dishes. These egg dishes are not only nutritious but also fun to make and eat. Remember, breakfast is an opportunity to start the day on a healthy note, so let's make it fun and exciting for the kids!

CHAPTER 4

LUNCHBOX HEROES

4.1 PACKED LUNCH IDEAS FOR DIABETIC KIDS

Packing a lunchbox for a child with diabetes can be a challenging task. It's not just about packing something delicious, but also ensuring that the meal is balanced and helps maintain stable blood sugar levels. Let's explore some packed lunch ideas that can make your child's lunchbox a hero.

The Needs of a Diabetic Child's Diet

A diabetic child's diet needs to be well-balanced, ensuring they get the right nutrients while maintaining their blood sugar levels. This requires careful selection of food items and portion control.

Packed Lunch Ideas for Diabetic Kids

Here are some packed lunch ideas that are both nutritious and delicious:

1. **Turkey & Cheese Sandwich**: Two whole wheat slices of bread contain 30 grams of carbohydrate. Add a fresh apple or peach, and you're up to 45 grams.

2. **Deconstructed Egg Salad**: Two hard-boiled eggs, carrot and celery sticks, and crackers. Make sure you get at least 30 grams of carbohydrate from the crackers and add a ready-to-go ½-cup of applesauce for a total of 45 grams.

3. **Chicken & Rice Soup**: A hearty serving of 1.5 cups has about 20 grams of carbohydrate. Include a side dish of your favorite crackers for another 15 grams, and a bunch of grapes for another 15 grams.

4. **BBQ Chicken Wrap**: One whole wheat tortilla contains about 20 grams of carbohydrate. Spread BBQ sauce, line with lettuce leaves, shredded carrots and onions, and tuck in 3 ounces of grilled chicken. Include a small box of raisins for dessert and you have a total of about 40 grams of carbohydrate.

5. **Hummus with Veggies**: One half (½) cup of hummus contains 20 grams of carbohydrate. You can use your favorite vegetable dippers or add a whole pita (25 grams of carbohydrate) and still be within the target range.

6. **Quick Pasta Salad**: Use some leftover pasta from dinner the night before. One cup will provide about 35 grams of carbohydrate. Toss in chopped veggies, cheese chunks, and drizzle with bottled Italian dressing. Finish off your lunch with a cup of strawberries (15 grams).

7. **Fried Rice**: Leftover rice from dinner makes an easy, quick reappearance as fried rice. Include whatever vegetables you have on hand (onion, celery, bell peppers, carrots, zucchini) and stir-fry with 1 egg. Sprinkle a small amount of teriyaki or soy sauce. One cup of white or brown rice contains 45 grams of carbohydrate.

8. **Yogurt Parfait**: Layer 1 cup of Greek yogurt, 1 cup of your favorite sliced fruit, and ¼ cup of granola.

Packing a lunchbox for a child with diabetes doesn't have to be a daunting task. With a little bit of planning and creativity, you can create meals that are both tasty and diabetes-friendly. Remember, every meal is an opportunity to nourish your child's body and manage their diabetes better. So, make every lunch count!

4.2 SANDWICHES AND WRAPS

When it comes to packing a lunchbox, sandwiches and wraps are the undisputed heroes. They are versatile, easy to make, and can be filled with a variety of nutritious ingredients. Let's explore some creative ideas for sandwiches and wraps that can make lunchtime exciting and delicious.

The Versatility of Sandwiches and Wraps

Sandwiches and wraps offer endless possibilities for creativity. With a variety of breads, fillings, and spreads to choose from, you can create a different combination every day.

Creative Sandwich Ideas

Here are some creative sandwich ideas that are sure to delight:

1. **Turkey Strawberry Wrap**: This wrap combines salty, smoked turkey with juicy strawberries and tangy poppy seed dressing for a unique flavor combination.

2. **Buffalo Chicken Wraps**: These wraps are full of buffalo chicken, creamy ranch dressing, crispy bacon, and chopped tomatoes. They're light enough for lunch and filling enough for dinner.

3. **Hummus Collard Wraps**: For a healthier alternative to traditional wraps, try using collard greens. These wraps can fit much more inside and are perfect with cold fillings like hummus, cucumber, and zucchini.

Innovative Wrap Ideas

Wraps offer a lighter alternative to sandwiches and can be just as versatile. Here are some innovative wrap ideas:

1. **Artichoke Steak Wraps**: This simple, fast, and flavorful dish is one the whole family loves. It's surprisingly easy to

make, and you can broil the steak if you don't want to venture outside[1].

2. **Cranberry Turkey Wraps**: These wraps are fruity and flavorful, with quick and easy sandwich wraps making any packed lunch delicious—and a breeze.

3. **Club Roll-Ups**: Packed with meat, cheese and olives, these sandwich wraps are always a hit at parties.

Sandwiches and wraps are the lunchbox heroes that never disappoint. They offer endless possibilities for creativity and can cater to every taste and dietary need. So, why not experiment with different combinations and discover your own lunchbox hero?

4.3 SALADS AND VEGGIE BOWLS

When it comes to packing a lunchbox, salads and veggie bowls are the unsung heroes. They are versatile, packed with nutrients, and can be customized to cater to individual tastes. Let's explore some creative ideas for salads and veggie bowls that can make lunchtime a healthy and delightful experience.

The Benefits of Salads and Veggie Bowls

Salads and veggie bowls are not just about leafy greens and raw vegetables. They can include a variety of ingredients like whole grains, lean proteins, and healthy fats. This makes them a balanced meal option that is both filling and nutritious.

Creative Salad Ideas

Here are some creative salad ideas that are sure to delight:

1. **Grain Bowl with Chickpeas & Cauliflower**: This beautiful grain bowl is packed with healthy ingredients like quinoa, chickpeas, kale, and cauliflower—all drizzled with a lemony tahini sauce.

2. **Meal-Prep Roasted Vegetable Bowls with Pesto**: Your co-workers will be jealous when you pull out this healthy lunch of roasted veggies and brown rice.

3. **Sweet Potato & Cauliflower Rice Bowl**: In this riff on a healthy grain bowl recipe, we use cauliflower rice instead of another whole grain like brown rice to cut back on carbs and load up on veggie servings.

Innovative Veggie Bowl Ideas

Veggie bowls offer a lighter alternative to heavy lunches and can be just as versatile. Here are some innovative veggie bowl ideas:

1. **Vegan Grain Bowl**: This easy grain bowl has so much to love—sweet potatoes, protein-packed chickpeas, creamy avocado, and homemade tahini dressing.

2. **Green Goddess Grain Bowl**: This healthy grain bowl packs in the greens with peas, asparagus, and a creamy yogurt dressing.

3. **Vegetarian Protein Bowl**: This vegetarian protein bowl has everything you need for a complete meal in one bowl.

Salads and veggie bowls are the lunchbox heroes that never disappoint. They offer endless possibilities for creativity and can cater to every taste and dietary need. So, why not experiment with different combinations and discover your own lunchbox hero?

4.4 HOMEMADE SOUPS

When it comes to packing a lunchbox, homemade soups often don't get the recognition they deserve. They are versatile, packed with nutrients, and can be customized to cater to individual tastes. Let's explore some creative ideas for homemade soups that can make lunchtime a warm and comforting experience.

Benefits of Homemade Soups

Homemade soups are not just about warmth and comfort. They can include a variety of ingredients like whole grains, lean proteins, and vegetables, making them a balanced meal option that is both filling and nutritious.

Creative Homemade Soup Ideas

Here are some creative homemade soup ideas that are sure to delight:

1. **Easy Homemade Vegetable Soup**: This hearty vegetable soup recipe is healthy, easy to make, and tastes fantastic. It's also vegan when a vegetable broth is used.

2. **Homemade Chicken Noodle Soup**: This comforting chicken noodle soup is a take on a soup many of us ate during childhood. It is loaded with ingredients to boost your immune system and can easily be made vegan or vegetarian.

3. **Homemade Vegetable Soup**: This soup is pretty close to what many of us used to make. It's always thought of as healthy and filling. There is no meat and very little fat in this recipe.

Innovative Homemade Soup Ideas

Homemade soups offer a lighter alternative to heavy lunches and can be just as versatile. Here are some innovative homemade soup ideas:

1. **Squash and Sage Soup**: This soup combines the sweetness of squash with the earthy flavor of sage, making it a unique and delightful dish.

2. **Easy Dutch Oven Minestrone Soup**: This soup is quick to prepare and is ready in less than an hour. Add a salad and a warm crusty loaf of bread to round out the meal.

3. **Ceylon Chicken Curry Noodle Soup**: This comforting chicken curry noodle soup is a take on a soup many of us ate during childhood. It is loaded with ingredients to boost your immune system and can easily be made vegan or vegetarian.

Homemade soups are the unsung heroes of lunchboxes. They offer endless possibilities for creativity and can cater to every taste and dietary need. So, why not experiment with different combinations and discover your own lunchbox hero?

CHAPTER 5

DINNER FAVORITES

5.1 WHOLESOME DINNERS FOR THE WHOLE FAMILY

Dinner is a time when families come together to share their day and enjoy a meal. But preparing a dinner that is both wholesome and appealing to the whole family can be a challenge. Let's explore some dinner favorites that are not only nutritious but also delicious.

Importance of Wholesome Dinners

A wholesome dinner is about more than just filling bellies. It's about providing the necessary nutrients for growth, energy, and overall health. It's also about creating meals that the whole family will enjoy.

Wholesome Dinner Ideas

Here are some wholesome dinner ideas that are sure to be a hit with the whole family:

1. **Turkey Meatball Lettuce Wraps**: These wraps are a healthier alternative to traditional meatball subs, using lean turkey meat and lettuce wraps instead of bread.

2. **Leek & Mushroom Chicken with Spaghetti Squash**: This dish offers a low-carb alternative to traditional pasta dishes, using spaghetti squash instead of pasta.

3. **Chicken Ktzitzot**: These Israeli-style chicken patties are flavorful and easy to make, making them a great option for a family dinner.

4. **Zucchini Lasagna**: This lasagna uses zucchini instead of pasta for a low-carb, veggie-packed dinner option.

5. **Vegetarian Moroccan Stuffed Peppers**: These stuffed peppers are filled with a flavorful mixture of couscous and veggies, making them a great vegetarian option.

6. **Red Roast Chicken with Vegetables**: This one-pot meal is easy to prepare and packed with flavor.

7. **Avocado Stuffed Salmon**: This dish combines the heart-healthy fats of avocado and salmon for a delicious and nutritious dinner.

Preparing wholesome dinners for the whole family doesn't have to be a daunting task. With a little bit of planning and creativity, you can create meals that are both nutritious and delicious. Remember, every meal is an opportunity to nourish your family's bodies and foster a love for healthy eating. So, make every dinner count!

5.2 ONE-POT MEALS

One-pot meals are the unsung heroes of the dinner table. They offer a world of convenience, flavor, and nutrition, all while keeping clean-up to a minimum. Let's explore some delightful one-pot meal ideas that can make dinner time a breeze.

The Appeal of One-Pot Meals

One-pot meals are about more than just convenience. They allow flavors to mingle and develop together, often resulting in dishes that are more flavorful and harmonious. Plus, they often require less time and effort, making them perfect for busy weeknights.

Delightful One-Pot Meal Ideas

Here are some delightful one-pot meal ideas that are sure to become dinner favorites:

1. **Chicken Pot Pie with Cheese Biscuit Topping**: This comforting dish combines the savory flavors of chicken pot pie with the cheesy goodness of biscuits, all baked together in one pot.

2. **Cajun Jambalaya**: This one-pot wonder is packed with flavor, featuring the holy trinity of Cajun cooking: onion, celery, and green bell pepper, along with andouille sausage.

3. **Spicy Pasta with Ground Beef and Tomatoes**: This hearty pasta dish is easy to make and packed with flavor, all cooked together in one pot for easy clean-up.

4. **Breakfast Casserole with Sausage, Eggs, and Biscuits**: Who says one-pot meals are only for dinner? This breakfast casserole is a delicious way to start the day.

5. **Cauliflower and Sausage Roast with Cheddar Cheese**: This low-carb one-pot meal is a complete meal in itself, featuring cauliflower, cheese, and sausage.

6. **Roasted Chicken Dinner with Potatoes**: This one-pot meal is a classic, featuring a whole chicken roasted with potatoes for a comforting and satisfying meal.

One-pot meals are the dinner heroes that save the day. They offer convenience, flavor, and nutrition, all while keeping clean-up to a minimum. So, why not experiment with different one-pot meals and discover your own dinner favorite? Remember, a delicious and nutritious dinner doesn't have to mean hours in the kitchen or a sink full of dishes.

5.3 PASTA AND WHOLE GRAIN DELIGHTS

Pasta and whole grains are versatile ingredients that can be the stars of many delightful dinner dishes. They are not only delicious but also packed with nutrients, making them a healthy choice for dinner. Let's explore some pasta and whole grain delights that can make dinner time a culinary adventure.

Benefits of Pasta and Whole Grains

Pasta and whole grains are rich in carbohydrates, providing the body with the energy it needs. Whole grains, in particular, are packed with fiber, vitamins, and minerals, making them a healthier choice compared to refined grains.

Delightful Pasta Dishes

Here are some delightful pasta dishes that are sure to become dinner favorites:

1. **Whole Grain Pasta with Roasted Vegetables**: This dish combines the nutty flavor of whole grain pasta with the sweetness of roasted vegetables.

2. **Pasta Primavera**: This classic pasta dish is packed with fresh vegetables and can be made with whole grain pasta for added nutrition.

3. **Spaghetti with Turkey Meatballs**: This dish is a healthier twist on the classic spaghetti and meatballs, using lean turkey meat and whole grain spaghetti.

Wholesome Whole Grain Dishes

Whole grains can be used in a variety of dishes. Here are some wholesome whole grain dishes:

1. **Quinoa Salad with Roasted Vegetables**: This salad is packed with protein-rich quinoa and a variety of roasted vegetables, making it a nutritious and filling meal.

2. **Brown Rice Stir-Fry**: This dish is a healthier version of the classic stir-fry, using fiber-rich brown rice.

3. **Barley and Mushroom Risotto**: This hearty dish uses pearl barley instead of rice, giving it a unique texture and a boost of fiber.

Pasta and whole grain dishes are dinner favorites that offer both taste and nutrition. They are versatile and can be used in a variety of dishes, making dinner time an exciting culinary adventure. Remember, a delicious and nutritious dinner is the perfect end to a day!

5.4 KID-FRIENDLY VEGETABLE DISHES

Getting kids to eat their veggies can sometimes be a challenge. But with a little creativity and a lot of flavors, vegetables can transform into kid-friendly dishes that are both delicious and nutritious. Let's explore some kid-friendly vegetable dishes that can make dinner time a fun and healthy experience.

Appeal of Kid-Friendly Vegetable Dishes

Kid-friendly vegetable dishes are about more than just nutrition. They're about creating meals that are colorful, fun, and tasty, making veggies more appealing to the little ones.

Delightful Vegetable Dishes

Here are some delightful vegetable dishes that kids will love:

1. **Kid-Friendly Pasta Salad**: This pasta salad is packed with lots of fresh veggies and pasta, making it a healthy, filling, colorful, and delicious dish that your child will love.

2. **Kid-Friendly Vegetable Roast**: This easy veggie roast is a great way to get kids to eat their veggies. It's colorful, fun to eat, and packed with flavor.

3. **Cauliflower Broccoli Casserole**: This casserole is a hit with kids, combining the flavors of cauliflower and broccoli with a creamy sauce.

4. **Baked Zucchini (Courgette) Fritters**: These fritters are a fun and tasty way to get kids to eat their veggies.

5. **Cheesy Zucchini Tots**: These tots are a healthier alternative to traditional tater tots, using zucchini instead of potatoes.

Innovative Vegetable Dishes

Here are some innovative vegetable dishes that kids will love:

1. **Cauliflower Bites in Honey Sriracha Sauce**: These cauliflower bites are a fun and tasty snack that kids will love.

2. **Veggie Faces**: This dish makes eating veggies fun by arranging them into fun faces.

3. **Baked Bell Pepper Tacos**: These tacos use bell peppers instead of taco shells for a fun and healthy twist.

Kid-friendly vegetable dishes are the dinner heroes that make veggies fun and tasty. They offer endless possibilities for creativity and can cater to every taste. So, why not experiment with different vegetable dishes and discover your own dinner favorite? Remember, a delicious and nutritious dinner is the perfect end to a day!

CHAPTER 6

SNACK ATTACK

6.1 HEALTHY SNACKING FOR DIABETIC KIDS

Snacking can be a crucial part of a child's diet, especially for those living with diabetes. It can help manage blood sugar levels and provide the necessary nutrients for growth and development. Let's explore some healthy snacking options that are both nutritious and appealing to kids.

Importance of Healthy Snacking

Healthy snacking is about more than just curbing hunger between meals. For diabetic kids, it's about maintaining stable blood sugar levels while also providing essential nutrients. This requires careful selection of snacks and understanding their impact on blood glucose levels.

Healthy Snack Ideas for Diabetic Kids

Here are some healthy snack ideas that are sure to be a hit with diabetic kids:

1. **Frozen, Low-Fat, No Sugar Yogurt or Ice-Cream**: These can be a great alternative to regular ice-cream, providing a sweet treat without the added sugar.

2. **Low-Fat Milk and Cheese**: Dairy products are a good source of calcium and protein, which are essential for growth.

3. **Apple Wedges and Grapes**: Fresh fruits are a great snack option. They are sweet, easy to eat, and packed with vitamins.

4. **Cherry Tomatoes or Banana Slices**: These can be a fun and colorful way to include vegetables in your child's diet.

5. **Unsweetened Fruit Juices**: These can be a refreshing alternative to sugary drinks.

6. **String Cheese with Crackers**: This is a kid-friendly snack that provides a good balance of protein and carbohydrates.

7. **Sugar-Free Pudding or Jello with Fresh Berries**: This can be a tasty treat that is low in sugar.

Healthy snacking is an essential part of managing diabetes in kids. It's about finding the balance between taste and nutrition. Remember, every snack is an opportunity to nourish your child's body and manage their diabetes better. So, make every snack count!

6.2 FRUIT AND NUT COMBOS

Fruit and nut combos are a delightful way to enjoy a snack or enhance a meal. They offer a balance of sweet and savory flavors, crunchy and soft textures, and a host of nutritional benefits. Let's explore some unique and delicious fruit and nut combinations that can elevate your culinary experience.

Appeal of Fruit and Nut Combos

Fruit and nut combos are about more than just taste. They offer a balance of essential nutrients, including fiber, protein, healthy fats, vitamins, and minerals. This makes them a wholesome choice for a snack or as an addition to meals.

Delightful Fruit and Nut Combos

Here are some delightful fruit and nut combos that are sure to tantalize your taste buds:

1. **Apple and Almonds**: The crispness of apples pairs well with the creaminess of almonds. This combo also offers a good balance of fiber from apples and protein from almonds.

2. **Apricot and Hazelnuts**: The sweet and slightly tart flavor of apricots complements the rich, nutty flavor of hazelnuts.

3. **Banana and Walnuts**: This classic combo is not only delicious but also packed with potassium from bananas and omega-3 fatty acids from walnuts.

4. **Cashews and Dried Cranberries**: The creaminess of cashews and slightly tart cranberries are a perfect match.

5. **Peanuts, Raisins, and Sunflower Seeds**: These are like the peanut butter & jelly of snacking - it's classic and everybody likes it.

Innovative Fruit and Nut Combos

For those who like to experiment with flavors, here are some innovative fruit and nut combos:

1. **Pomegranate and Pistachios**: The sweet and tart arils of pomegranate pair beautifully with the rich, slightly sweet flavor of pistachios.

2. **Pear and Pine Nuts**: The soft, sweet flavor of pears is enhanced by the buttery flavor of pine nuts.

3. **Mango and Macadamia Nuts**: The tropical sweetness of mangoes and the rich, buttery flavor of macadamia nuts make for a delightful combo.

Fruit and nut combos are a delightful way to enjoy a snack or enhance a meal. They offer a symphony of flavors and a host of nutritional benefits. So, why not experiment with different fruit and nut combos and discover your own favorite?

6.3 GUILT-FREE DESSERTS

Desserts are often associated with guilt due to their high sugar and calorie content. However, it's possible to enjoy desserts without the guilt by making healthier choices. Let's explore some guilt-free dessert recipes that are as delicious as they are nutritious.

Concept of Guilt-Free Desserts

Guilt-free desserts are about more than just cutting calories. They're about incorporating wholesome ingredients that add nutritional value, reducing refined sugars, and focusing on portion control.

Delightful Guilt-Free Desserts

Here are some delightful guilt-free desserts that you can enjoy without the guilt:

1. **Strawberry Cheesecake**: This guilt-free dessert is high in vitamin C and only contains 138 calories per serving.

2. **Banana Pudding**: This dessert is very low in fat and contains only 102 calories per serving.

3. **Quinoa Almond Joy Bars**: These bars are packed with protein and fiber and contain only 94 calories per serving.

4. **Raspberry Oat Bars**: These bars are packed with antioxidants from berries and contain 212 calories per serving.

5. **Frothy Chocolate Shake**: This shake is loaded with protein and calls for homemade chocolate syrup. It contains 269 calories per serving.

6. **Skinny Strawberry Ice Cream**: Made with only four ingredients, two of which are superfoods, this ice cream contains 116 calories per serving.

Innovative Guilt-Free Desserts

For those who like to experiment with flavors, here are some innovative guilt-free desserts:

1. **Slow Cooker Cranberry Poached Pears**: This dessert is high in fiber and contains 224 calories per serving.

2. **Chocolate Pudding**: This pudding is high in antioxidants and contains 283 calories per serving.

3. **Piña Colada Pops**: These pops are low in sugar and contain no refined sugar. They contain 182 calories per serving.

4. **Fudge Brownie Bites**: These bites are sweetened with fiber-packed dates and contain 124 calories per serving.

5. **Clean Eating Almond Butter Fudge**: This fudge is rich in antioxidants and heart-healthy fats. It contains 129 calories per serving.

Guilt-free desserts allow you to satisfy your sweet tooth without the guilt. They offer a balance of taste and nutrition, making them a delightful end to any meal. So, why not experiment with guilt-free desserts and discover your own favorite?

6.4 FUN AND TASTY FINGER FOODS

Finger foods are the unsung heroes of the culinary world. They are versatile, fun to eat, and can cater to a variety of tastes. Let's explore some fun and tasty finger food ideas that can make your next gathering a culinary adventure.

Appeal of Finger Foods

Finger foods are about more than just convenience. They offer a unique dining experience, allowing you to sample a variety of flavors and textures in one sitting.

Delightful Finger Foods

Here are some delightful finger foods that are sure to be a hit at your next gathering:

1. **Deviled Potato Bites**: These bite-sized potato cups are filled with a creamy and tangy mixture of mashed potatoes, sour cream, and spices, topped with crispy bacon and chives.

2. **Rosemary Steak Bites**: Have your wine and eat it, too, with this easy appetizer. Fresh rosemary functions as both flavor and a DIY skewer.

3. **Buffalo Chicken Football Hand Pies**: Score a touchdown with these savory and spicy buffalo chicken football hand pies, packed with flavorful buffalo chicken and creamy blue cheese.

4. **Jalapeño Poppers**: I swear my brain unlocked a new level the day I learned that jalapeño poppers were this easy to make.

5. **Shrimp and Avocado Tostadas**: They might be crispy and easy to break, but I wouldn't be surprised if you finish these off in one bite each.

Innovative Finger Foods

For those who like to experiment with flavors, here are some innovative finger foods:

1. **Creamy Spinach-Stuffed Mushrooms**: A mixture of cream cheese, butter, spinach, and Parmesan cheese means each

bite of these mushroom cups will be a savory, buttery explosion of flavor.

2. **Chicken Satay Skewers**: Skewers can be bland and boring. Thankfully, that's not the case for these little guys, which are marinated in a spicy coconut milk- and peanut butter-based sauce.

3. **Cheesy Chicken Balls**: Shredding the chicken into tiny pieces means these balls will be easy to form and maintain their shape.

4. **Toasted Ravioli**: Dredging and frying your ravioli in oil instead of simply boiling it transforms this simple pasta into a crispy appetizer.

5. **Pigs in Blankets**: Just because you discovered pigs in blankets as a child doesn't mean you can't enjoy them as an adult.

Finger foods are the culinary heroes that make dining a delightful experience. They offer endless possibilities for creativity and can cater to every taste. So, why not experiment with different finger foods and discover your own culinary adventure?

CHAPTER 7

SWEETS AND TREATS

7.1 SUGAR-FREE DESSERT RECIPES

In the world of desserts, the word "sugar-free" often raises eyebrows. Can desserts be delicious without the sweet allure of sugar? The answer is a resounding yes! Let's embark on a culinary journey exploring the realm of sugar-free desserts.

The Sugar-Free Revolution

Sugar has long been the undisputed champion of sweetness in our desserts. However, with the rise in health consciousness and dietary restrictions, we've started to see a shift towards healthier alternatives. Sugar-free desserts are not just for those with dietary restrictions or health concerns; they're for anyone who wants to enjoy a sweet treat without the guilt.

The Magic of Natural Sweeteners

Who said sugar-free means taste-free? Nature is abundant with sweet miracles like fruits, honey, and even some vegetables. These natural sweeteners can provide the sweetness we crave, without the negative effects of refined sugar. For instance, ripe bananas or dates can add a rich, caramel-like sweetness to your desserts, while honey or maple syrup can provide a subtle, nuanced flavor.

Delicious Sugar-Free Dessert Recipes

Let's dive into some mouth-watering sugar-free dessert recipes that you can easily whip up at home:

1. **Banana Ice Cream**: All you need are ripe bananas! Slice them, freeze them, and blend them. You'll end up with a creamy, naturally sweet ice cream that's 100% sugar-free.

2. **Date Brownies**: Dates are nature's candy. Blend them with nuts and cocoa powder, and voila! You have a batch of delicious, sugar-free brownies.

3. **Apple Crumble**: Sweet, tart apples topped with a crunchy oat-nut crumble. Use a touch of honey or maple syrup to sweeten the deal.

4. **Chia Pudding**: Chia seeds, almond milk, and a touch of honey or stevia come together to create a pudding that's both healthy and satisfying.

Sugar-free desserts are a fantastic way to satisfy your sweet tooth without the guilt. They're proof that you can have your cake (sugar-free, of course!) and eat it too. So why not give these recipes a try? You might just find your new favorite dessert!

7.2 BAKING WITH ALTERNATIVE SWEETENERS

In the world of baking, sugar has long reigned supreme. But what if we told you that there's a whole world of alternative sweeteners out there, waiting to be explored? Let's take a journey into the world of baking with alternative sweeteners.

The Rise of Alternative Sweeteners

As we become more health-conscious, many of us are looking for ways to reduce our sugar intake. This is where alternative sweeteners come in. They offer the sweetness we crave, without the calories and health risks associated with refined sugar.

Exploring the Alternatives

There's a wide range of alternative sweeteners available, each with its own unique flavor profile and baking properties. Here are a few of our favorites:

1. **Honey**: This natural sweetener is not only delicious but also offers a host of health benefits. It's great for moist cakes and bread.

2. **Maple Syrup**: With its rich, caramel-like flavor, maple syrup is a fantastic alternative for baked goods like cookies and pies.

3. **Stevia**: This zero-calorie sweetener is derived from a plant and is much sweeter than sugar, so you'll need less of it.

4. **Dates**: These sweet fruits can be pureed and used as a natural sweetener in a variety of baked goods.

Baking with Alternative Sweeteners: Tips and Tricks

Baking with alternative sweeteners can be a bit tricky, as they don't behave exactly like sugar. Here are a few tips to help you get started:

- Start small: When substituting sugar with an alternative sweetener, start with a small amount and adjust to taste.

- Consider the texture: Some sweeteners can affect the texture of your baked goods. For example, honey can make your cakes more moist.

- Experiment: Don't be afraid to try different sweeteners and see what works best for your recipe.

Baking with alternative sweeteners can open up a whole new world of flavors and textures. It's all about experimenting and finding what works for you. So why not give it a try? You might just discover a new favorite recipe! Happy baking!

7.3 INDULGENT YET HEALTHY TREATS

In the world of culinary delights, the term "healthy" often conjures up images of bland salads and tasteless snacks. But what if we told you that indulgence and health can go hand in hand? Let's explore the world of indulgent yet healthy treats.

The Art of Healthy Indulgence

Healthy indulgence is all about balance. It's about finding ways to enjoy the foods we love in a way that also nourishes our bodies. This might sound like a tall order, but with a little creativity and a few key ingredients, it's entirely possible.

Key Ingredients for Healthy Indulgence

Here are a few ingredients that can transform your treats from guilty pleasures to healthy indulgences:

1. **Dark Chocolate**: Packed with antioxidants, dark chocolate can satisfy your sweet tooth while also providing health benefits.

2. **Nuts and Seeds**: These are not only delicious but also packed with healthy fats and protein.

3. **Fruits**: Nature's candy, fruits add natural sweetness and a host of nutrients to your treats.

Indulgent yet Healthy Treat Recipes

Now, let's dive into some recipes that embody the spirit of healthy indulgence:

1. **Dark Chocolate Covered Strawberries**: Melt some dark chocolate, dip in fresh strawberries, and chill. It's a simple yet decadent treat that's also healthy.

2. **Almond Butter Stuffed Dates**: Slice open a date, fill it with almond butter, and you have a treat that's both sweet and satisfying.

3. **Frozen Banana Ice Cream**: Blend frozen bananas until smooth, and you have a creamy, healthy alternative to traditional ice cream.

Indulgent yet healthy treats are not a myth, but a reality waiting to be explored in your kitchen. With the right ingredients and a bit of creativity, you can savor the flavor without the guilt. So why not give these recipes a try? You might just find your new favorite treat! Happy indulging!

7.4 CELEBRATING SPECIAL OCCASIONS

In the tapestry of life, special occasions are the vibrant threads that add color and meaning. They bring us together, help us create memories, and add a touch of magic to the everyday. Let's explore the art of celebrating special occasions.

The Importance of Celebrating Special Occasions

Special occasions are milestones that mark significant moments in our lives. They give us a chance to pause, reflect, and celebrate our achievements, relationships, and personal growth. Whether it's a birthday, an anniversary, or a graduation, each occasion is a chapter in our life's story.

Creating Memorable Celebrations

Creating a memorable celebration doesn't necessarily mean extravagant parties or expensive gifts. It's about making the day special for the person or people involved. Here are a few tips:

1. **Personalize**: Tailor the celebration to the person's interests and preferences. A personalized celebration shows thoughtfulness and care.

2. **Create Traditions**: Traditions can add a sense of continuity and anticipation to special occasions. They can be as simple as a special breakfast on birthdays or a yearly family picnic.

3. **Capture the Moment**: Photos, videos, and keepsakes can help preserve the memory of the special day.

Celebrating in a Digital Age

In today's digital age, we have more ways than ever to celebrate special occasions. Virtual parties, video messages, and online gift exchanges are just a few of the ways we can connect and celebrate with loved ones, no matter the distance.

Celebrating special occasions is about more than just marking time. It's about honoring our journey, expressing our love for others, and creating memories that last a lifetime. So, whether it's a small gathering at home or a virtual celebration, remember to make it meaningful, personal, and most importantly, enjoyable! After all, these are the moments that make life truly special.

CHAPTER 8

BEVERAGES AND HYDRATION

8.1 SUGAR-FREE DRINK OPTIONS

In the beverage landscape, sugar-laden drinks often take center stage. But what if we told you that there's a whole world of sugar-free drink options that are not only refreshing but also healthful? Let's dive into this thirst-quenching topic.

The Sugar-Free Shift

As we become more health-conscious, many of us are looking for ways to reduce our sugar intake. This is where sugar-free drinks come in. They offer the hydration and flavor we crave, without the calories and health risks associated with refined sugar.

Exploring Sugar-Free Drink Options

There's a wide range of sugar-free drink options available, each with its own unique flavor profile and health benefits. Here are a few of our favorites:

1. **Water**: The ultimate sugar-free drink. It's essential for our health and can be spruced up with a slice of lemon or cucumber for added flavor.

2. **Herbal Tea**: From chamomile to peppermint, herbal teas offer a variety of flavors without the need for sugar.

3. **Vegetable Juice**: Freshly squeezed vegetable juices are a great way to stay hydrated and get a dose of vitamins and minerals.

4. **Sparkling Water**: If you miss the fizz of sugary sodas, sparkling water is a great alternative.

Making the Switch to Sugar-Free Drinks

Switching to sugar-free drinks doesn't have to be a daunting task. Start by gradually reducing the amount of sugar in your beverages. Experiment with different sugar-free options and find what you enjoy the most.

Sugar-free drinks are a fantastic way to stay hydrated and healthy. They're proof that you can enjoy a refreshing beverage without the guilt. So why not give these options a try? You might just find your new favorite drink! Cheers to a healthier, sugar-free lifestyle!

8.2 HYDRATION TIPS FOR DIABETIC KIDS

Living with diabetes as a child can be challenging, but with the right guidance and knowledge, it's entirely manageable. One crucial aspect of managing diabetes is staying properly hydrated. Let's delve into some hydration tips for diabetic kids.

Importance of Hydration

Hydration plays a vital role in our overall health. For diabetic kids, it's even more critical. High blood sugar levels can lead to dehydration, making it essential for kids with diabetes to consume adequate fluids throughout the day.

Hydration Tips for Diabetic Kids

Here are some practical tips to ensure diabetic kids stay well-hydrated:

1. **Regular Fluid Intake**: Encourage regular drinking of fluids throughout the day, not just when they're thirsty.

2. **Choose Water**: Water should be the primary source of hydration. It's sugar-free and helps maintain blood sugar levels.

3. **Limit Sugary Drinks**: Sugary drinks can cause blood sugar levels to spike. Opt for sugar-free alternatives when possible.

4. **Monitor Blood Sugar Levels**: Regular monitoring can help identify if the child is dehydrated, as high blood sugar levels can be a sign of dehydration.

Hydration and Exercise

Exercise is essential for kids with diabetes, but it can also lead to dehydration. Ensure they drink plenty of water before, during, and after physical activity.

Staying hydrated is a crucial part of managing diabetes in children. With these tips, you can help ensure that your child maintains proper hydration, supporting their overall health and well-being. Remember, managing diabetes is a team effort, and with the right strategies, your child can lead a healthy, balanced life.

8.3 CREATIVE MOCKTAILS AND SMOOTHIES

In the realm of beverages, mocktails and smoothies hold a special place. They offer a delightful blend of flavors, colors, and textures, making them a hit among people of all ages. Let's dive into the world of creative mocktails and smoothies.

The Art of Crafting Mocktails

Mocktails, or non-alcoholic cocktails, are all about creativity and presentation. They allow you to experiment with a variety of ingredients, from fresh fruits and herbs to sparkling water and flavored syrups. Here are a few creative mocktail ideas:

1. **Citrus Twist**: A refreshing blend of fresh orange, lemon, and lime juices, topped with sparkling water and garnished with a slice of citrus fruit.

2. **Berry Blast**: A vibrant mix of muddled fresh berries, lemon juice, and honey, served over crushed ice.

3. **Tropical Paradise**: A tropical delight featuring pineapple juice, coconut milk, and a dash of grenadine for that sunset hue.

Smoothies: A Blend of Health and Taste

Smoothies are not just delicious, they're also a great way to pack in a bunch of nutrients. From fruits and vegetables to yogurt and nuts, the possibilities are endless. Here are a few creative smoothie ideas:

1. **Green Goddess**: A nutrient-packed smoothie with spinach, avocado, green apple, and a hint of mint.

2. **Berry Banana Bonanza**: A classic combination of strawberries, blueberries, and bananas, blended with a dollop of Greek yogurt.

3. **Choco-Nut Delight**: A decadent yet healthy smoothie featuring bananas, almond milk, cocoa powder, and a spoonful of almond butter.

Mocktails and smoothies offer a world of flavors waiting to be explored. They're a testament to the fact that healthy and tasty can indeed go hand in hand. So why not don your creative hat and whip up these delightful beverages? Happy blending!

CHAPTER 9

MEAL PLANNING AND PORTION CONTROL

9.1 IMPORTANCE OF MEAL PLANNING

In the hustle and bustle of our daily lives, meal planning often takes a backseat. But did you know that planning your meals can have a significant impact on your health, budget, and lifestyle? Let's delve into the importance of meal planning.

Why Meal Planning Matters

Meal planning is more than just deciding what to eat. It's about making conscious decisions about what we put into our bodies. Here's why it matters:

1. **Nutrition**: Meal planning ensures that we get a balanced diet with all the necessary nutrients.

2. **Budget**: Planning meals in advance can help save money by reducing impulsive take-out orders and minimizing food waste.

3. **Time**: With meals planned, we can streamline grocery shopping and cooking, saving valuable time.

The Art of Meal Planning

Meal planning is an art that can be mastered with a bit of practice. Here are some tips to get you started:

1. **Start Small**: If you're new to meal planning, start with planning just a few meals a week.

2. **Consider Your Schedule**: Plan your meals according to your weekly schedule. Save complex recipes for when you have more time.

3. **Prep in Advance**: Prepare ingredients or entire meals ahead of time to make cooking easier.

Meal Planning and Portion Control

Meal planning goes hand in hand with portion control, a key aspect of maintaining a healthy weight and managing dietary needs. By planning meals, we can ensure that our portions are balanced and suitable for our dietary needs.

Meal planning is a powerful tool that can transform our relationship with food. It puts us in control of our diet, health, and budget. So why not give meal planning a try? You might just find it to be a game-changer in your journey towards a healthier lifestyle.

9.2 PORTION CONTROL TIPS FOR KIDS

Portion control is about understanding and choosing the right amount of food to consume. It's a vital part of a balanced diet and plays a crucial role in preventing overeating and promoting healthy growth in children.

Portion Control Tips for Kids

Here are some effective strategies to help your child understand and practice portion control:

1. **Use Visual Aids**: Visual aids can be a fun and effective way to teach kids about portion sizes. For instance, a serving of fruit could be the size of a tennis ball, while a serving of meat could be the size of a deck of cards.

2. **Serve Smaller Portions**: Start with smaller portions on your child's plate. They can always ask for more if they're still hungry.

3. **Encourage Mindful Eating**: Teach your child to eat slowly and pay attention to their hunger and fullness cues. This can prevent overeating and help them develop a healthier relationship with food.

4. **Lead by Example**: Children learn by observing. Practice portion control yourself and your child is likely to follow suit.

The Role of Meal Planning

Meal planning can be a great tool for portion control. By planning meals, you can ensure that your child gets a balanced diet with appropriate portion sizes.

Teaching portion control to kids is an investment in their future health. It's about equipping them with the knowledge and habits they need to make healthy food choices. Remember, it's not about restriction, but about balance and moderation. With these tips, you can help your child develop a healthy relationship with food that will last a lifetime.

9.3 CREATING BALANCED MEALS

Portion control is about understanding and choosing the right amount of food to consume. It's a vital part of a balanced diet and plays a crucial role in preventing overeating and promoting healthy growth in children.

Portion Control Tips for Kids

Here are some effective strategies to help your child understand and practice portion control:

1. **Use Visual Aids**: Visual aids can be a fun and effective way to teach kids about portion sizes. For instance, a serving of fruit could be the size of a tennis ball, while a serving of meat could be the size of a deck of cards.

2. **Serve Smaller Portions**: Start with smaller portions on your child's plate. They can always ask for more if they're still hungry.

3. **Encourage Mindful Eating**: Teach your child to eat slowly and pay attention to their hunger and fullness cues. This

can prevent overeating and help them develop a healthier relationship with food.

4. **Lead by Example**: Children learn by observing. Practice portion control yourself and your child is likely to follow suit.

The Role of Meal Planning

Meal planning can be a great tool for portion control. By planning meals, you can ensure that your child gets a balanced diet with appropriate portion sizes.

Teaching portion control to kids is an investment in their future health. It's about equipping them with the knowledge and habits they need to make healthy food choices. Remember, it's not about restriction, but about balance and moderation. With these tips, you can help your child develop a healthy relationship with food that will last a lifetime.

9.4 INVOLVING KIDS IN MEAL PREPARATION

In the bustling kitchen of life, involving kids in meal preparation can be a delightful blend of fun, learning, and bonding. It's an opportunity to teach them about nutrition, portion control, and the joy of creating something with their own hands. Let's explore this delicious topic.

The Benefits of Involving Kids in Meal Preparation

Involving kids in meal preparation has numerous benefits:

I. **Educational**: Kids learn about different foods, their nutritional value, and the importance of a balanced diet.

2. **Skills Development**: They acquire important skills like measuring, following instructions, and understanding time.

3. **Promotes Healthy Eating**: When kids participate in cooking, they're more likely to eat what they've helped prepare, including fruits and vegetables.

4. **Boosts Confidence**: Successfully preparing a meal can give kids a sense of accomplishment and boost their confidence.

Tips for Involving Kids in Meal Preparation

Here are some tips to make the experience enjoyable and safe:

1. **Start Simple**: Begin with simple tasks like washing vegetables or stirring ingredients.

2. **Teach Kitchen Safety**: Make sure they understand the importance of kitchen safety, including handling knives and hot surfaces.

3. **Be Patient**: Allow for mistakes and messes. It's all part of the learning process.

4. **Make it Fun**: Turn meal preparation into a fun activity. Play some music, involve them in menu planning, or create theme nights.

Meal Planning and Portion Control

Involving kids in meal planning and teaching them about portion control is a great way to instill healthy eating habits. They can learn about the different food groups, the importance of variety, and how to serve appropriate portions.

Involving kids in meal preparation is a wonderful way to spend quality time together, while also teaching them valuable life skills. It's about more than just cooking; it's about creating memories, fostering healthy habits, and savoring the joy of shared experiences. So, why not invite your little ones into the kitchen for your next meal preparation? The results might surprise you!

CHAPTER 10

STAYING ACTIVE AND HEALTHY

10.1 EXERCISE AND DIABETES

In the journey towards health and wellness, exercise plays a pivotal role, especially for individuals managing diabetes. Regular physical activity can have profound effects on blood sugar control and overall health. Let's delve into the dynamic relationship between exercise and diabetes.

The Impact of Exercise on Diabetes

Exercise is a powerful tool for managing diabetes. It helps in:

1. **Blood Sugar Control**: Regular physical activity can help lower blood sugar levels and improve your body's sensitivity to insulin.

2. **Weight Management**: Exercise aids in maintaining a healthy weight, which is crucial in managing diabetes.

3. **Heart Health**: Regular physical activity can help lower the risk of heart disease, a common concern for individuals with diabetes.

Incorporating Exercise into Your Routine

Here are some tips to help incorporate exercise into your daily routine:

1. **Start Slow**: If you're new to exercise, start with low-intensity activities like walking or swimming.

2. **Consistency is Key**: Aim for at least 30 minutes of moderate-intensity exercise most days of the week.

3. **Mix It Up**: Include a mix of cardio, strength training, and flexibility exercises in your routine.

Exercise Safely

When exercising with diabetes, safety should be a priority. Here are some safety tips:

1. **Monitor Blood Sugar**: Check your blood sugar levels before, during, and after exercise to prevent hypoglycemia.

2. **Stay Hydrated**: Drink plenty of fluids to stay hydrated.

3. **Wear Proper Footwear**: To prevent foot injuries, wear comfortable, well-fitting shoes.

Exercise and diabetes management go hand in hand. Regular physical activity can help manage blood sugar levels, promote weight loss, and improve overall health. Remember, it's important to start slow, be consistent, and prioritize safety. With these strategies, exercise can become an enjoyable and beneficial part of your diabetes management plan.

10.2 FUN PHYSICAL ACTIVITIES FOR KIDS

In the vibrant world of childhood, physical activity plays a crucial role. It's not just about staying active; it's about learning, exploring, and having fun. Let's dive into some fun physical activities that can keep kids active and engaged.

The Importance of Physical Activity for Kids

Physical activity is a key ingredient in the recipe for a healthy and happy childhood. It helps in:

1. **Physical Development**: Regular physical activity aids in the development of strong bones and muscles.

2. **Cognitive Development**: It enhances cognitive skills and improves concentration.

3. **Emotional Well-being**: Physical activity can boost mood and promote better sleep.

Fun Physical Activities for Kids

Here are some fun physical activities that kids can enjoy:

1. **Dance Party**: Turn on some music and let the kids show off their moves. Dancing is a great way to stay active and have fun.

2. **Nature Walks**: Exploring the outdoors can be an adventure. It's a great way to get some exercise and learn about nature.

3. **Bike Rides**: Biking is a fun and effective way to stay active. It also provides an opportunity to explore the neighborhood.

4. **Treasure Hunts**: Set up a treasure hunt in your backyard or park. It's a fun way to keep kids moving and engaged.

Making Physical Activity a Part of Daily Life

Incorporating physical activity into daily life doesn't have to be a chore. Make it fun and varied to keep kids interested. Encourage them to try different activities and find what they enjoy the most.

Physical activity is a vital part of childhood. It's about more than just health; it's about creating memories, learning new skills, and enjoying the sheer joy of movement. So why not incorporate these fun physical activities into your child's routine? They might just find a new favorite pastime!

10.3 ENCOURAGING A HEALTHY LIFESTYLE

In the vast landscape of life, maintaining a healthy lifestyle is a journey, not a destination. It's about making choices that contribute to our physical, mental, and emotional well-being. Let's explore how we can encourage a healthy lifestyle.

A Healthy Lifestyle

A healthy lifestyle is a way of living that lowers the risk of being seriously ill or dying early. It's not just about eating a balanced diet and exercising regularly, but also about taking care of our mental health and making time for relaxation and fun.

Components of a Healthy Lifestyle

A healthy lifestyle typically includes:

1. **Balanced Diet**: Consuming a variety of foods from all food groups in the right proportions.

2. **Regular Exercise**: Engaging in physical activity regularly to maintain fitness and health.

3. **Adequate Rest**: Ensuring enough sleep and relaxation to allow the body and mind to repair and rejuvenate.

4. **Positive Mindset**: Maintaining a positive outlook and managing stress effectively.

Encouraging a Healthy Lifestyle: Tips and Strategies

Here are some tips to encourage a healthy lifestyle:

1. **Lead by Example**: Show others how it's done by living a healthy lifestyle yourself.

2. **Educate**: Share information about the benefits of a healthy lifestyle and the risks of unhealthy habits.

3. **Make it Fun**: Turn healthy habits into enjoyable activities. For example, turn exercise into a game or cooking into a creative experiment.

4. **Provide Support**: Encourage others in their journey towards a healthy lifestyle and celebrate their achievements.

Encouraging a healthy lifestyle is about inspiring ourselves and others to make choices that promote well-being. It's about fostering an environment where health and wellness are valued and pursued. Remember, every step taken towards a healthier lifestyle, no matter how small, is a step in the right direction.

10.4 BUILDING HEALTHY HABITS FOR LIFE

In the grand architecture of life, healthy habits are the pillars that support our well-being. They are the routines we follow, the choices we make, and the disciplines we uphold. Let's explore how to build healthy habits for life.

Healthy Habits

Healthy habits are behaviors that enrich our physical, mental, and emotional health. These habits improve our overall well-being and make us feel good. They range from the foods we eat, the amount of exercise we get, to how we manage stress.

The Power of Healthy Habits

Healthy habits are powerful tools that can impact our health in numerous ways:

1. **Prevent Disease**: Regular exercise, a balanced diet, and adequate sleep can help prevent chronic diseases.

2. **Boost Mental Health**: Healthy habits like meditation, reading, and maintaining social connections can enhance mental health.

3. **Improve Longevity**: Studies show that the practice of healthy habits can prolong life expectancy.

Building Healthy Habits: A Step-by-Step Guide

Building healthy habits doesn't happen overnight. It's a process. Here are some steps to guide you:

1. **Start Small**: Focus on one or two habits at a time. Start with small, achievable goals.

2. **Consistency is Key**: Consistency is more important than intensity. It's better to walk every day for 30 minutes than to run a marathon once a year.

3. **Make it Enjoyable**: Choose activities that you enjoy. If you enjoy doing something, you're more likely to stick with it.

4. **Be Patient**: Change takes time. Don't get discouraged if you don't see immediate results.

Building healthy habits for life is a journey of self-discovery and commitment. It's about making choices that respect your body, mind, and spirit. Remember, the goal is not perfection, but progress. So, take that first step towards building your healthy habits today. Your future self will thank you!

SECTION B

DIABETES DIET DISHES

This are meals that are specifically designed for individuals managing diabetes. These dishes are typically prepared with a focus on maintaining balanced blood sugar levels.

SWEET POTATO WEDGES

Introduction: Have you ever craved something sweet, savory, and super healthy all at the same time? Meet our Sweet Potato Wedges! I chose this recipe because it's not only delicious but also diabetes-friendly. Sweet potatoes are packed with fiber and nutrients, making them a perfect snack or side dish. Plus, this recipe is so simple, even kids can join in the fun of making it!

Ingredients List:

- 2 large sweet potatoes

- 1 tablespoon olive oil

- ½ teaspoon paprika

- ¼ teaspoon garlic powder

- Salt and pepper, to taste

- A sprinkle of cinnamon (optional)

Preparation Steps:

1. Preheat your oven to 400°F (200°C).

2. Wash the sweet potatoes thoroughly and cut them into wedges.

3. In a large bowl, mix the sweet potato wedges with olive oil, paprika, garlic powder, salt, and pepper. Add a sprinkle of cinnamon if you like a hint of sweetness.

4. Spread the wedges out on a baking sheet in a single layer.

5. Bake in the oven for about 25-30 minutes, or until they are golden and slightly crispy. Halfway through, flip the wedges for even cooking.

Serving Size: This recipe serves about 4 people.

Nutritional Information (per serving):

- Calories: 103

- Carbohydrates: 17g

- Protein: 2g

- Fat: 3g

- Fiber: 3g

- Sugar: 4g

Tips:

- Feel free to experiment with different spices like cumin or a dash of chili powder for a bit of a kick.

- These wedges are fantastic when dipped in a low-fat Greek yogurt sauce or your favorite healthy dip.

- Remember, you can adjust the portion size to suit your dietary needs.

- Try using an air fryer for an even crispier texture!

Enjoy your Sweet Potato Wedges as a nutritious, diabetes-friendly treat that's fun to make and even more fun to eat!

MIXED BERRY SALAD WITH HONEY LIME DRESSING

Introduction: Ever wanted a dessert that's sweet, tangy, and bursting with colors? Our Mixed Berry Salad with Honey Lime Dressing is just that! I picked this recipe because it's a delightful mix of natural sweetness and zesty flavors, perfect for a refreshing snack or dessert. Berries are a fantastic choice for anyone, especially those following a diabetes-friendly diet. They're naturally sweet, so you won't miss the added sugars!

Ingredients List:

- 1 cup strawberries, hulled and halved

- 1 cup blueberries

- 1 cup raspberries

- 2 tablespoons honey (or a diabetes-friendly sweetener)

- Juice of 1 lime

- Fresh mint leaves for garnish (optional)

Preparation Steps:

1. In a large bowl, gently combine the strawberries, blueberries, and raspberries.

2. In a small bowl, whisk together the honey and lime juice until well mixed.

3. Drizzle the honey lime dressing over the berries and toss lightly to coat.

4. Garnish with fresh mint leaves for an added refreshing touch.

Serving Size: Serves 4 people.

Nutritional Information (per serving):

- Calories: 80

- Carbohydrates: 19g

- Protein: 1g

- Fat: 0.5g

- Fiber: 4g

- Sugar: 14g (natural sugars from berries)

Tips:

- You can mix and match with your favorite berries or whatever is in season.

- For a diabetes-friendly version, replace honey with a sweetener like stevia or just enjoy the natural sweetness of the berries.

- This salad is a perfect topping for low-fat Greek yogurt or whole-grain pancakes.

- Serve immediately after dressing to maintain the freshness and avoid soggy berries.

QUINOA VEGGIE STIR-FRY

Introduction: Are you in the mood for something both hearty and healthy? Our Quinoa Veggie Stir-Fry is here to save your dinner time! I selected this recipe because quinoa is a superfood that's not only good for you but also incredibly versatile and tasty. Combined with a colorful array of vegetables, this dish is a nutrient powerhouse that's perfect for anyone looking to enjoy a balanced, diabetes-friendly meal.

Ingredients List:

- I cup quinoa
- 2 cups water
- I tablespoon olive oil
- I small onion, chopped
- I bell pepper, diced
- I zucchini, sliced
- I carrot, sliced
- 2 cloves garlic, minced
- 2 tablespoons low-sodium soy sauce or tamari
- Salt and pepper, to taste
- Fresh herbs (like parsley or cilantro), for garnish

Preparation Steps:

I. Rinse the quinoa under cold water. In a saucepan, combine quinoa and water. Bring to a boil, then reduce heat, cover, and simmer for about 15 minutes until the quinoa is cooked and water is absorbed.

2. In a large skillet, heat the olive oil over medium heat. Add the onion and garlic, and sauté until fragrant.

3. Add the bell pepper, zucchini, and carrot. Cook, stirring occasionally, until the vegetables are tender.

4. Stir in the cooked quinoa and soy sauce. Season with salt and pepper. Cook everything together for a few more minutes.

5. Garnish with fresh herbs before serving.

Serving Size: Serves 4 people.

Nutritional Information (per serving):

- Calories: 220

- Carbohydrates: 39g

- Protein: 8g

- Fat: 5g

- Fiber: 5g

- Sugar: 3g

Tips:

- Feel free to add any other vegetables you love or have on hand, like broccoli, peas, or spinach.

- For extra protein, consider adding grilled chicken or tofu to the stir-fry.

- Quinoa comes in various colors like white, red, and black. Mix them up for a fun and colorful dish.

- Leftovers make a great lunch for the next day, as the flavors continue to meld together.

This Quinoa Veggie Stir-Fry isn't just a meal; it's a celebration of health, flavor, and color on your plate. Enjoy it as a fulfilling main dish that'll leave you satisfied and energized!

GREEK YOGURT PARFAIT WITH NUTS AND HONEY

Introduction: Looking for a sweet treat that's also good for you? Our Greek Yogurt Parfait with Nuts and Honey is the perfect choice! I love this recipe because Greek yogurt is a creamy, delightful base that pairs wonderfully with the crunch of nuts and the natural sweetness of honey. It's a simple yet luxurious snack or breakfast that's easy to make and can be customized to your liking.

Ingredients List:

- 1 cup Greek yogurt (plain, low-fat)

- 2 tablespoons honey (or a diabetic-friendly sweetener)

- ¼ cup mixed nuts (almonds, walnuts, pecans), chopped

- Optional: fresh berries or a sprinkle of cinnamon

Preparation Steps:

1. In a serving bowl or glass, layer half of the Greek yogurt.

2. Drizzle with 1 tablespoon of honey (or sweetener) and sprinkle half of the chopped nuts over the yogurt.

3. Add the remaining Greek yogurt on top of the nuts.

4. Finish with the remaining honey and nuts. If you're using berries or cinnamon, add them on top for extra flavor and color.

Serving Size: Serves 1.

Nutritional Information (per serving):

- Calories: 320

- Carbohydrates: 35g

- Protein: 20g

- Fat: 12g

- Fiber: 2g

- Sugar: 28g (natural sugars from yogurt and honey)

Tips:

- For a lower sugar content, use a diabetic-friendly sweetener instead of honey.

- You can add fresh fruit like strawberries, blueberries, or bananas for extra nutrients and fiber.

- Experiment with different nuts or seeds (like chia seeds or pumpkin seeds) for varied textures and flavors.

- If you're looking for a vegan option, use plant-based yogurt and a vegan sweetener.

This Greek Yogurt Parfait with Nuts and Honey is not just a dish; it's a delightful, nutritious experience. It's perfect for a quick breakfast, a post-workout snack, or even a dessert that won't spike your blood sugar. Enjoy this creamy, crunchy, and sweet delight guilt-free!

SPINACH AND FETA STUFFED CHICKEN BREAST

Introduction: Fancy a dish that's as nutritious as it is delicious? Our Spinach and Feta Stuffed Chicken Breast is a fantastic combination of lean protein and leafy greens. I chose this recipe because it's a wonderful way to incorporate spinach into your diet in a flavorful and satisfying manner. The rich taste of feta cheese complements the mild, earthy flavor of spinach perfectly, making this dish a hit for both adults and kids!

Ingredients List:

- 4 boneless, skinless chicken breasts

- 2 cups fresh spinach, chopped

- ½ cup feta cheese, crumbled

- 2 cloves garlic, minced

- 1 tablespoon olive oil

- Salt and pepper, to taste

- Optional: a pinch of dried oregano or basil

Preparation Steps:

1. Preheat your oven to 375°F (190°C).

2. In a pan, heat the olive oil over medium heat. Add the garlic and spinach, cooking until the spinach wilts. Remove from heat and let it cool slightly.

3. Mix the wilted spinach with feta cheese. Add salt, pepper, and optional herbs to taste.

4. Make a pocket in each chicken breast by cutting along the side. Stuff each breast with the spinach and feta mixture.

5. Place the stuffed chicken breasts in a baking dish. Season the outside with salt and pepper.

6. Bake for 25-30 minutes, or until the chicken is cooked through and no longer pink in the middle.

Serving Size: Serves 4 people.

Nutritional Information (per serving):

- Calories: 230

- Carbohydrates: 2g

- Protein: 30g

- Fat: 11g

- Fiber: 1g

- Sugar: 1g

Tips:

- You can add chopped sun-dried tomatoes or olives to the stuffing for an extra flavor boost.

- If you're not a fan of feta, try using goat cheese or mozzarella instead.

- Serve with a side of roasted vegetables or a fresh salad for a complete meal.

- For an extra golden and crispy exterior, you can sear the chicken breasts in a pan before baking.

This Spinach and Feta Stuffed Chicken Breast is not just a meal; it's a celebration of healthy eating. It's a delicious way to enjoy a balanced diet, perfect for anyone keeping an eye on their blood sugar without sacrificing flavor. Bon appétit!

MEDITERRANEAN OLIVE OIL AND GARLIC SPAGHETTI

Introduction: Craving a pasta dish that's both heart-healthy and full of flavor? Our Mediterranean Olive Oil and Garlic Spaghetti is a simple yet elegant dish that brings the essence of the Mediterranean to your table. I chose this recipe because olive oil is a staple of heart-healthy diets, and when combined with garlic, it creates a deliciously aromatic and light sauce for pasta. It's a dish that's both comforting and nutritious, perfect for any day of the week!

Ingredients List:

- 8 oz whole grain spaghetti

- ¼ cup extra virgin olive oil

- 4 cloves garlic, thinly sliced

- A pinch of red pepper flakes (optional)

- Salt and black pepper, to taste

- 2 tablespoons fresh parsley, chopped

- Grated Parmesan cheese, for serving (optional)

Preparation Steps:

1. Cook the spaghetti according to package instructions until al dente. Drain and set aside, reserving a little pasta water.

2. In a large skillet, heat the olive oil over medium heat. Add the sliced garlic and red pepper flakes. Cook until the garlic is golden and fragrant, being careful not to burn it.

3. Add the cooked spaghetti to the skillet. Toss well to coat the pasta in the olive oil and garlic. If the pasta seems dry, add a little of the reserved pasta water.

4. Season with salt and black pepper to taste. Stir in the chopped parsley.

5. Serve hot, sprinkled with grated Parmesan cheese if desired.

Serving Size: Serves 4 people.

Nutritional Information (per serving):

- Calories: 320

- Carbohydrates: 45g

- Protein: 8g

- Fat: 13g

- Fiber: 6g

- Sugar: 2g

Tips:

- You can add sautéed vegetables like bell peppers, cherry tomatoes, or spinach for a more nutritious and colorful dish.

- For added protein, consider topping with grilled chicken, shrimp, or cannellini beans.

- Opt for whole grain pasta for its higher fiber content, which is better for blood sugar control.

- Remember, while olive oil is healthy, it's also high in calories, so use it in moderation.

This Mediterranean Olive Oil and Garlic Spaghetti is a testament to how simple ingredients can create a meal that's both delicious and healthy. It's perfect for those looking to enjoy classic flavors while managing their diabetes. Enjoy this light and satisfying dish any day of the week!

ROASTED CHICKPEA AND VEGGIE SALAD

Introduction: Looking for a salad that's hearty, nutritious, and full of flavor? Our Roasted Chickpea and Veggie Salad is just the ticket! I love this recipe because chickpeas add a satisfying crunch and protein punch, making this salad a filling and healthy meal. Combined with a variety of roasted vegetables, it's a colorful and delicious way to enjoy a range of nutrients.

Ingredients List:

- 1 can (15 oz) chickpeas, drained and rinsed

- 1 zucchini, chopped

- 1 bell pepper, chopped

- 1 red onion, chopped

- 2 tablespoons olive oil

- 1 teaspoon paprika

- Salt and pepper, to taste

- Mixed greens (like spinach, arugula, and lettuce)

- For the dressing: 2 tablespoons balsamic vinegar, 1 tablespoon olive oil, 1 teaspoon Dijon mustard

Preparation Steps:

1. Preheat your oven to 400°F (200°C).

2. In a bowl, toss the chickpeas with 1 tablespoon olive oil, paprika, salt, and pepper. Spread on a baking sheet.

3. On another baking sheet, toss the chopped zucchini, bell pepper, and red onion with the remaining olive oil, salt, and pepper.

4. Roast the chickpeas and vegetables in the oven for 20-25 minutes until the chickpeas are crispy and the vegetables are tender.

5. Prepare the dressing by whisking together balsamic vinegar, olive oil, and Dijon mustard.

6. In a large bowl, combine the mixed greens with the roasted vegetables and chickpeas.

7. Drizzle the dressing over the salad and toss to combine.

Serving Size: Serves 4 people.

Nutritional Information (per serving):

- Calories: 250

- Carbohydrates: 35g

- Protein: 9g

- Fat: 10g

- Fiber: 9g

- Sugar: 7g

Tips:

- Feel free to add other roasted vegetables like carrots, broccoli, or cauliflower.

- For extra protein, top the salad with grilled chicken, tofu, or feta cheese.

- The roasted chickpeas can also be a great snack on their own.

- You can store the leftover roasted chickpeas and veggies in the fridge for an easy meal prep option.

This Roasted Chickpea and Veggie Salad is a perfect example of how a simple meal can be both delicious and nutritionally balanced. It's ideal for anyone looking for a tasty way to manage their diabetes with food. Enjoy this delightful salad packed with flavor and health benefits!

CINNAMON APPLE CHIPS

Introduction: Craving a sweet, crunchy snack that's both healthy and easy to make? Our Cinnamon Apple Chips are the perfect solution! I chose this recipe because it's a delightful way to enjoy the natural sweetness of apples, enhanced with a hint of cinnamon. These apple chips are a fantastic snack for any time of the day and are a hit with both kids and adults.

Ingredients List:

- 2 large apples (any variety, but Fuji or Gala work well)

- 1 teaspoon ground cinnamon

- A sprinkle of sugar or sugar substitute (optional)

Preparation Steps:

1. Preheat your oven to 200°F (95°C).

2. Wash the apples and thinly slice them, discarding the seeds and core.

3. Arrange the apple slices in a single layer on a baking sheet lined with parchment paper.

4. Sprinkle the slices with cinnamon and a touch of sugar or sugar substitute, if using.

5. Bake for 1-2 hours, flipping the slices halfway through, until they are dry and crisp.

6. Let them cool completely before serving, as they will crisp up more as they cool.

Serving Size: Makes about 4 servings.

Nutritional Information (per serving):

- Calories: 50

- Carbohydrates: 13g

- Protein: 0g

- Fat: 0g

- Fiber: 2g

- Sugar: 10g (natural sugars from apples)

Tips:

- Experiment with different apple varieties to find your favorite flavor.

- Be sure to slice the apples thinly for the perfect crispness.

- These apple chips can be stored in an airtight container for a few days.

- For a different flavor, try sprinkling with a little nutmeg or pumpkin spice.

CLASSIC TOMATO BRUSCHETTA

Introduction: In the mood for something light, fresh, and full of flavor? Our Classic Tomato Bruschetta is a delightful choice! This recipe is a celebration of simplicity, featuring ripe tomatoes at their best. It's a perfect appetizer or snack that's not only delicious but also diabetes-friendly, thanks to the low-carb profile of tomatoes.

Ingredients List:

- 4 large ripe tomatoes, diced

- 1 clove garlic, minced

- 1 tablespoon extra-virgin olive oil

- 1 teaspoon balsamic vinegar

- Fresh basil leaves, chopped

- Salt and pepper, to taste

- Whole grain baguette, sliced and toasted

Preparation Steps:

1. In a mixing bowl, combine the diced tomatoes, minced garlic, olive oil, and balsamic vinegar.

2. Add the chopped basil, salt, and pepper to the tomato mixture. Gently toss to combine.

3. Let the mixture sit for about 10-15 minutes to allow flavors to meld.

4. Spoon the tomato mixture generously onto the toasted baguette slices.

Serving Size: Serves 4-6 people as an appetizer.

Nutritional Information (per serving, without baguette):

- Calories: 45

- Carbohydrates: 6g

- Protein: 1g

- Fat: 2g

- Fiber: 1g

- Sugar: 4g

Tips:

- Choose the ripest, most flavorful tomatoes you can find for the best taste.

- For a garlic-infused flavor, rub a halved garlic clove on the toasted baguette slices before topping them with the tomato mixture.

- You can add a sprinkle of cheese, like mozzarella or feta, for extra flavor.

- For a low-carb option, serve the bruschetta topping over grilled chicken breasts or a bed of mixed greens.

OVERNIGHT OATS WITH BERRIES AND NUTS

Introduction: Fancy a breakfast that's not only delicious but also ready when you wake up? Our Overnight Oats with Berries and Nuts is the perfect solution! I love this recipe because it's incredibly easy to prepare, and oats are a fantastic, low-glycemic base for a nutritious meal. Topped with berries for sweetness and nuts for crunch, this breakfast is a delightful way to start your day.

Ingredients List:

- I cup rolled oats

- I cup unsweetened almond milk (or any milk of your choice)

- ½ cup Greek yogurt

- I tablespoon chia seeds

- I tablespoon honey or a diabetic-friendly sweetener

- ½ cup mixed berries (like blueberries, strawberries, raspberries)

- ¼ cup mixed nuts, chopped (almonds, walnuts, pecans)

Preparation Steps:

1. In a bowl or jar, combine the rolled oats, almond milk, Greek yogurt, chia seeds, and honey or sweetener.

2. Mix well until all the ingredients are fully combined.

3. Cover the bowl or jar and refrigerate overnight (or at least 6 hours).

4. In the morning, give the oats a good stir. If they're too thick, add a little more milk to reach your desired consistency.

5. Top the oats with mixed berries and chopped nuts before serving.

Serving Size: Serves 2 people.

Nutritional Information (per serving):

- Calories: 345

- Carbohydrates: 45g

- Protein: 15g

- Fat: 14g

- Fiber: 9g

- Sugar: 12g

Tips:

- Customize your overnight oats with your favorite fruits, nuts, and seeds.

- For added flavor, stir in a pinch of cinnamon or vanilla extract.

- If you prefer a warmer breakfast, you can heat the oats in the microwave before adding the toppings.

- Remember to use rolled oats, as they absorb liquid well and create a creamy texture.

These Overnight Oats with Berries and Nuts are not just a meal; they're a nutritious, delicious, and convenient way to enjoy a balanced breakfast. It's perfect for busy mornings and a great start to a day for anyone, especially those managing diabetes. Enjoy this no-fuss, tasty, and healthy breakfast!

CAULIFLOWER FRIED RICE

Introduction: Ever wanted a healthier version of your favorite fried rice? Our Cauliflower Fried Rice is here to satisfy your cravings! I chose this recipe because cauliflower is a fantastic low-carb alternative to rice, and it soaks up flavors beautifully. This dish is packed with veggies and is a flavorful, nutritious option for anyone looking to enjoy a classic comfort food in a healthier way.

Ingredients List:

- 1 medium head of cauliflower, grated or processed into rice-sized pieces

- 2 tablespoons sesame oil

- 1 small onion, diced

- 1 cup mixed vegetables (carrots, peas, bell peppers)

- 2 cloves garlic, minced

- 2 eggs, lightly beaten

- 2 tablespoons low-sodium soy sauce or tamari

- Salt and pepper, to taste

- Green onions, chopped, for garnish

Preparation Steps:

1. Grate the cauliflower using a box grater or pulse it in a food processor until it resembles rice.

2. Heat one tablespoon of sesame oil in a large pan or wok over medium heat. Sauté the onion and garlic until fragrant.

3. Add the mixed vegetables to the pan and cook until tender.

4. Push the veggies to one side of the pan, add the remaining sesame oil, and pour in the beaten eggs. Scramble the eggs and then mix with the vegetables.

5. Add the cauliflower "rice" to the pan. Pour the soy sauce over the top and stir everything together. Cook for 5-7 minutes, or until the cauliflower is tender.

6. Season with salt and pepper to taste. Garnish with chopped green onions.

Serving Size: Serves 4 people.

Nutritional Information (per serving):

- Calories: 150

- Carbohydrates: 15g

- Protein: 7g

- Fat: 7g

- Fiber: 4g

- Sugar: 5g

Tips:

- Feel free to add any other vegetables you like or have on hand.

- For added protein, you can include diced chicken, shrimp, or tofu.

- If you're in a hurry, you can use pre-processed cauliflower rice available in most grocery stores.

- For a soy-free version, use coconut aminos instead of soy sauce.

This Cauliflower Fried Rice is not just a dish; it's a healthy twist on a classic favorite. It's perfect for those managing diabetes or anyone looking for a lighter, yet satisfying meal. Enjoy the flavors and textures of this delightful, nutritious alternative to traditional fried rice!

GRILLED CHICKEN SALAD WITH MIXED GREENS

Introduction: Craving something light yet protein-packed? Our Grilled Chicken Salad with Mixed Greens is a perfect choice! I selected this recipe because it combines the lean goodness of grilled chicken with the freshness of mixed greens and a variety of vegetables. It's a healthy, flavorful, and satisfying meal that's ideal for anyone, especially those managing diabetes.

Ingredients List:

- 2 boneless, skinless chicken breasts
- 1 tablespoon olive oil
- Salt and pepper, to taste
- 4 cups mixed greens (like spinach, arugula, and romaine)
- 1 cucumber, sliced
- 1 bell pepper, sliced
- 10 cherry tomatoes, halved
- 2 tablespoons balsamic vinaigrette

Preparation Steps:

1. Preheat your grill or grill pan over medium heat.
2. Brush the chicken breasts with olive oil and season with salt and pepper.
3. Grill the chicken for about 6-7 minutes on each side, or until it's fully cooked and has nice grill marks.

4. Let the chicken rest for a few minutes, then slice it into strips.

5. In a large bowl, combine the mixed greens, cucumber, bell pepper, and cherry tomatoes.

6. Add the grilled chicken to the salad.

7. Drizzle with balsamic vinaigrette and toss gently to combine.

Serving Size: Serves 2-3 people.

Nutritional Information (per serving):

- Calories: 250

- Carbohydrates: 8g

- Protein: 26g

- Fat: 12g

- Fiber: 3g

- Sugar: 4g

Tips:

- You can add other vegetables like shredded carrots or red onion for extra crunch and flavor.

- For a different taste, try using lemon juice and herbs like rosemary or thyme to season the chicken.

- If you prefer, you can substitute the chicken with other lean meats like turkey or even grilled fish.

- Adding a sprinkle of nuts or seeds (like almonds or sunflower seeds) can add a nice texture.

BLACK BEAN AND CORN SALSA

Introduction: Fancy a dip that's as nutritious as it is delicious? Our Black Bean and Corn Salsa is a vibrant and flavorful choice! I love this recipe because it combines the heartiness of black beans with the sweetness of corn, creating a perfect balance of flavors. It's a versatile dish that can be served as a dip, a side, or even as a topping for grilled meats or fish.

Ingredients List:

- 1 can (15 oz) black beans, rinsed and drained
- 1 cup corn kernels (fresh, canned, or thawed from frozen)
- 1 medium tomato, diced
- 1 small red onion, finely chopped
- 1 jalapeño, seeded and minced (optional)
- ¼ cup fresh cilantro, chopped
- Juice of 1 lime
- Salt and pepper, to taste

Preparation Steps:

1. In a large bowl, combine the black beans, corn, diced tomato, red onion, and jalapeño (if using).
2. Add the chopped cilantro and squeeze in the lime juice.
3. Season with salt and pepper to taste.
4. Stir everything together until well combined.
5. Let the salsa sit for about 15 minutes to allow the flavors to meld together.

Serving Size: Serves 4-6 as a side or appetizer.

Nutritional Information (per serving):

- Calories: 120

- Carbohydrates: 22g

- Protein: 6g

- Fat: 1g

- Fiber: 6g

- Sugar: 3g

Tips:

- If you prefer a little heat, leave the seeds in the jalapeño or add a dash of hot sauce.

- This salsa is great served with whole grain tortilla chips or as a topping for grilled chicken or fish.

- For added color and nutrition, mix in diced bell peppers or avocado.

- The salsa can be stored in the refrigerator for up to 3 days, making it a great make-ahead option.

ZUCCHINI NOODLES WITH PESTO AND CHERRY TOMATOES

Introduction: Looking for a light yet satisfying dish that's full of flavor? Our Zucchini Noodles with Pesto and Cherry Tomatoes is an excellent choice! I adore this recipe because zucchini noodles (also known as "zoodles") are a fantastic low-carb alternative to traditional pasta. Paired with homemade pesto and juicy cherry tomatoes, this dish is a delightful blend of fresh, vibrant flavors.

Ingredients List:

- 2 medium zucchinis
- 1 cup cherry tomatoes, halved
- ½ cup basil leaves
- 2 cloves garlic
- ¼ cup pine nuts
- ¼ cup grated Parmesan cheese
- ¼ cup olive oil
- Salt and pepper, to taste

Preparation Steps:

1. Use a spiralizer or a vegetable peeler to turn the zucchinis into noodles. Set aside.

2. In a food processor, blend basil leaves, garlic, pine nuts, and Parmesan cheese. Gradually add olive oil until the mixture becomes a smooth pesto. Season with salt and pepper.

3. In a large bowl, toss the zucchini noodles with the pesto sauce until well coated.

4. Gently mix in the halved cherry tomatoes.

5. Serve immediately, or chill in the refrigerator if you prefer a colder dish.

Serving Size: Serves 2-3 people.

Nutritional Information (per serving):

- Calories: 210

- Carbohydrates: 10g

- Protein: 6g

- Fat: 18g

- Fiber: 3g

- Sugar: 5g

Tips:

- If you don't have a spiralizer, a vegetable peeler can create thin, pasta-like strips of zucchini.

- Feel free to add other vegetables like spinach or bell peppers to the mix.

- For a vegan version, substitute the Parmesan with nutritional yeast.

- Toasting the pine nuts before blending can add extra flavor to the pesto.

STUFFED BELL PEPPERS WITH QUINOA AND VEGETABLES

Introduction: Craving something hearty yet healthy? Our Stuffed Bell Peppers with Quinoa and Vegetables are a perfect pick! I chose this recipe because it's a fantastic way to enjoy the sweetness of bell peppers, combined with the nutty flavor of quinoa and the freshness of veggies. It's a colorful, nutritious meal that's as pleasing to the eye as it is to the palate.

Ingredients List:

- 4 bell peppers (any color), tops cut off and seeds removed
- 1 cup cooked quinoa
- 1 tablespoon olive oil
- 1 small onion, diced
- 2 cloves garlic, minced
- 1 zucchini, diced
- 1 carrot, diced
- ½ cup corn kernels (fresh or frozen)
- 1 can (15 oz) black beans, rinsed and drained
- 1 teaspoon ground cumin
- Salt and pepper, to taste
- Shredded cheese for topping (optional)

Preparation Steps:

1. Preheat your oven to 375°F (190°C).

2. In a skillet, heat the olive oil over medium heat. Add the onion and garlic, sautéing until soft.

3. Add the zucchini, carrot, and corn to the skillet. Cook for a few minutes until the vegetables are tender.

4. Stir in the cooked quinoa, black beans, cumin, salt, and pepper. Cook for another 2-3 minutes.

5. Spoon the quinoa and vegetable mixture into each bell pepper.

6. Place the stuffed peppers in a baking dish and cover with foil.

7. Bake for 25-30 minutes, until the peppers are tender. Remove the foil, add cheese on top if desired, and bake for an additional 5 minutes.

Serving Size: Serves 4 people.

Nutritional Information (per serving):

- Calories: 250

- Carbohydrates: 40g

- Protein: 10g

- Fat: 7g

- Fiber: 10g

- Sugar: 8g

Tips:

- You can use any color of bell pepper – each has a slightly different flavor.

- Feel free to add other vegetables or a protein source like ground turkey or tofu to the stuffing.

- For a cheesy flavor without the extra fat, sprinkle nutritional yeast on top instead of cheese.

- Leftover stuffing can be used the next day as a salad topper or in a wrap.

VEGGIE-PACKED FRITTATA

Introduction: In the mood for a protein-rich and flavorful meal? Our Veggie-Packed Frittata is just what you need! I love this recipe because it's a wonderful way to incorporate a variety of vegetables into your diet, along with the wholesome goodness of eggs. It's a flexible dish that can be enjoyed any time of the day - breakfast, lunch, or dinner.

Ingredients List:

- 6 large eggs

- 1/4 cup milk (or dairy-free alternative)

- Salt and pepper, to taste

- 2 tablespoons olive oil

- 1 small onion, diced

- 1 red bell pepper, diced

- 1 cup spinach, roughly chopped

- 1 medium zucchini, sliced

- 1/2 cup cherry tomatoes, halved

- 1/4 cup grated cheese (optional)

Preparation Steps:

1. Preheat your oven to 375°F (190°C).

2. In a bowl, whisk together the eggs, milk, salt, and pepper.

3. Heat olive oil in an oven-safe skillet over medium heat. Sauté the onion and bell pepper until soft.

4. Add the spinach and zucchini to the skillet, cooking until the spinach wilts.

5. Pour the egg mixture over the vegetables. Scatter the cherry tomatoes on top.

6. Cook on the stove for a few minutes until the edges start to set.

7. Sprinkle grated cheese on top, if using.

8. Transfer the skillet to the oven and bake for 10-15 minutes, until the frittata is set and golden.

Serving Size: Serves 4-6 people.

Nutritional Information (per serving):

- Calories: 140

- Carbohydrates: 5g

- Protein: 10g

- Fat: 9g

- Fiber: 1g

- Sugar: 3g

Tips:

- You can use any combination of vegetables you have on hand, like mushrooms, asparagus, or broccoli.

- For a dairy-free version, omit the cheese or use a plant-based cheese alternative.

- Leftovers can be stored in the refrigerator and make a great quick meal or snack.

- Serve the frittata with a side salad or whole grain toast for a complete meal.

THE END